THE SCOTTISH AMBASSADOR

THE SCOTTISH AMBASSADOR

Robert Crawford

CAPE POETRY

1 3 5 7 9 10 8 6 4 2

Jonathan Cape, an imprint of Vintage,
20 Vauxhall Bridge Road,
London SW1V 2SA

Jonathan Cape is part of the Penguin Random House group of companies
whose addresses can be found at global.penguinrandomhouse.com

Penguin
Random House
UK

First published by Jonathan Cape in 2018

penguin.co.uk/vintage

A CIP catalogue record for this book is available
from the British Library

ISBN 9781787330689

Typeset in 11/13 pt Bembo by Jouve (UK), Milton Keynes
Printed and bound in Great Britain by TJ International Ltd, Padstow, Cornwall

Penguin Random House is committed to a sustainable future for
our business, our readers and our planet. This book is made
from Forest Stewardship Council® certified paper.

for Alice, Lewis, and Blyth
with love

CONTENTS

SEARCH

Right now, as the Zoroaster of Fife,
The Lower Largo Noah,

I want to bid you hop aboard
This vessel built in my yard,

Part fast and bonny *Hispaniola*,
Part old duffer's old puffer:

Sextant to hand, help me start
Our maiden voyage, on which, I grant,

You'll never budge from this paper-thin deck,
Circling the globe like *Gipsy Moth*,

Becoming at once an armchair Viking,
A Dampier, a Magellan,

Taking your bearings from an ongoing search
Of Nineveh, Edinburgh, Hong Kong, all

Tabulated in this vessel's log
In language almost but not quite yours,

As you take the wheel for a while at least,
Steering our ark home under the stars,

Allowing for the vagaries of navigation
And the distance, the closeness between us.

WAIT

Sit.
Do nothing

But wait.
It may

Or may not
Come again.

You must just
Stay, waiting

As in a concert interval cellos
And double basses

And violin cases
Stay on,

Strewn in the pit
Like corpses, the musicians all gone.

PARSI

Just hold out your arms
To the sun. Stand. Feel your wrists
Pulsing with worship.

FIRE

In your heart
Start to construct

A stripped
Zoroastrian temple,

To contain,
Then release, the flame;

Invoke again
The phosphoric Name,

Calling to the fire,
Let it speak back

By night
In impatient match-heads,

By day
As a burning man;

Let it complain
About its crackling lack,

Blurting out
Its *I am*

Through the held look,
The confession in the loins,

All things
Are measured by fire,

4

As the blaze lurches, sings,
And soars,

A burning
Kestrel,

Then perches
On charred beams,

Or roars
Its red shout

As it joins,
Soft and molten,

The living procession,
Vestal.

PRIMER

Wooed by flame,
Let it teach you its grammar
So you know and parse it
As it knows and parses you,

And let it teach, too,
Its explosive sums,
How fire's one and one
Equals one.

HANGING BALCONY,
JERUSALEM

for Leena Nammari

Stand
In old age
On tired feet,
Dizzy
With grieving,
In that tall,
Filigree cage
Hung
On the wall
Above the busy,
Unwavering street,
And peer out
Through diesel stink
And heat
At the small,
Blistered land,
Then hear the young
Call
Of a quavering voice
Prompt you to think
Day
After day
About making a choice
About leaving,
About learning to stay.

THE READING LIGHT

At daybreak
As Columba woke
To fasting,
Then throughout that day
An intensely bright
Everlasting
Light
Sheathed him, and shone
Through keyholes,
Through chinks
Round doors,
As if kindled
In a hearth
At the heart
Of that Iona house
While all day long
Columba sang
New songs
Never
Heard till then
And became aware
Of secrets hidden
Since before
The start
Of the world,
And he mastered the art
Of how to handle
Difficult scriptures,
Making clear
Their hymnlike core,
Their simple
Inner candle.

after the Latin of Adomnán, Vita Sancti Columbae, III, 18

ALL LABOURERS' HELPER

after the Latin attributed to St Columba

All labourers' helper,
Blessèd men's ruler,
Chief ramparts' warder,
Deep faith's defender,
Each small man's lifter,
Fashion-plates' humbler,
Great navigator,
Heretic-crusher,
Just judges' judger,
Keen sinners' punisher,
Light of good-livers,
Man's sanctifier,
New illuminator,
O endless giver,
Perfect in vigour,
Quicken my prayer;
Receive it, Master,
So, though I am no braver
Than the weakest rower
Under loud thunder's
Violent clamour,
Welcome me to the Father's
'X' – Christ the Keeper's
Yearned-for Cross. Saviour,
Zealously may you conquer
Per dominum nostrum
Forever and ever.

SMALL DATA

Road, stroll with me now
To the west-coast machair. Road,
Take my breath away.

*

It is a real place,
But its weather, its seasons
Are a Book of Hours.

*

As it was for saints,
So for us too, the world is
Data – given things.

*

The smallest data
Make everything bend here,
Make us nod assent.

*

Soon at the Four Roads,
Eyes on the sea and fast clouds,
I will take the fifth.

SEARCH ENGINE

It's made up of the Chinese game of Go
And the verb *ogle*

And is itself a noun turned verb – a nerb –
A sly nerd verb

Whose servers gobble megawatts, like secret cities.
It data-mines money. It is power,

Stalking, clocking us, our digital legacy,
Oracle of all our porn,

Meaning a huge number, like the word legion,
A speed-of-light centurion swarm.

Your house is there, your partner is there, your dreams are there.
Go on, enter your name.

ARS POETICA

On the fine line between genius and pretentiousness
I try to land on the side of pretentiousness.
That way, I know if I make a blunder
My work will be acclaimed forever.

LEVITY

Baghdad of the West, gallimaufry of Zahahadidery,
Heavy with locos, liners, yards and docks
Docked now of shipyards, sculpted, purled into shining
Titanium hulls where Wild West meets West End,
Your square-bashing sandstone Kremlin an offcut of Venice,
Your galleries a showy clone of Santiago de Compostella,
One-off of sugar and gallusness, Adam Smith and preening baroque,
Art-schooled from birth, ark, blast-furnace of ship-in-bottle
Models and artwork, arsenic, scuffed footballs and chips,
Unsafe haven of hard matriarchs and lasses' backchat, after-hours
Capital of banana boots and over-the-top porcelain fountains,
Wannabe Paris, pre-Chicago Chicago,
Fifty-first state of glottal-stopped, reeling smirr
In Helen of Troy rainhoods, your Charles Rennie Mackintosh brooch
Fogged with drizzle, champagned with Victorian catarrh;
Tenemented redoubt of roll-ups, landed with God's geology
To use as your doormat, viridian lochs and bens,
Renaissance anvil of spires and boot-scrapers, Scotia Bar of bards,
Gay hardmen's last stand, palace of perished velveteens,
All second-city edginess, fossil grove, puddled panache,
Operatic, fat, incessantly jumpy with static,
Gralloching yourself, tearing yourself apart
To hit back through lesions or drooled ferro-concrete bridges,
Jokes and spread-betting, canals, class war and bombs
Flung by staunch hunger-strikers, polis of asbestos spit,
Morphing into a stained-glassed, ran-dan, ram-stam disco
Of theme-pub banks intact with mahogany counters,
Gothic lavvies, high flats, giddy deserts wi windaes
Looking out on the lashing, softening, incoming rain
Of tomorrow, its wetness honeycombed in glasshouses,
Tobacco Lords and dry Snell Exhibitioners, fish that never swam,
Inner-city dolphins glimpsed off the starboard side,

Spanish Civil War fighters, Gorbals Lascars and lazars,
Lens-sellers, subway keelies, bibliographers
Bowling on bowling greens or strolling to Bowling or high
In library corridors hoisted by gaunt, spinal cranes
Seen from the Green, that Champs-Élysées of peely-wally faces
Hungry for *liberté, égalité, fraternité*
In all their forms, despite the imperial sweat
Of plunder they profited from, the feared years of tears and blood
Shed at home in domestic violence, Cath-Prod slashings, and away
Mismatches in thin red lines that still hurt, but can't stop
The levity that's yours and yours alone and will last
Longer than Horatian bronze just because it's laughter.

FULL MOON

The clear, round clockface,
Amputated of its hands,
Will last forever.

PROFESSOR

Back when the noun *hack* was stained with printer's ink,
Long before the days of printer ink,

When *drones* meant pibroch or P. G. Wodehouse
I remember sitting in the English Language

Classroom, observing Professor Samuels,
Chesty author of *Linguistic Evolution*,

Mummified with several striped, hand-knitted
Scarves against the Glasgow climate,

Unbinding himself from his mufflers.
Beady-eyed, Pharaonic, he came alive

Explaining how the word *silly* for Chaucer
Meant *innocent*, and quoting Noam Chomsky

On *colourless green ideas*. His masterpiece,
His dream, *The Historical Thesaurus of English*,

Involved recombining all the definitions
Of the *Oxford English Dictionary*

To show how, across the centuries, words
Had added to or addled their meanings.

We laughed to hear how the first *typewriters*
Were marriageable, like the earliest *computers*,

As we sat, taking notes on glottal stops,
Listening to that Anglo-Tusitala,

That seismographer of etymology,
Who made us feel proud we had never received

Received Pronunciation. I noticed you, Alice,
In that wonderland of vowel shifts and drifting phonemes,

And fell in love, though it took me years
To find the right words. We recognised

Each other among those semantic shifts
And that blur of competing voices,

Just as, today, for all he's been dead
Ten years, when we catch his bookish name,

We still recognise Professor Samuels,
Pipe-cleaner-thin with his scarves and briefcase,

That punning matchmaker of the English language,
Passing from a bank where the wild thyme blows

Past a bank of phonetics-lab reel-to-reels
To the Bank of Scotland, Sauchiehall Street.

MENU

In a succulence of warm September rain
We are the *amuse bouche*, we are the main.

CAMERA OBSCURA

Nae knickers, all fur coat
Slurped Valvona and Crolla,
Tweed-lapelled, elbow-patched, tartan-skirted,
Kilted, Higgs-bosoned, tramless, trammelled and trammed,
Awash with drowned witches prematurely damned,
Prim as skimmed milk, cheesily floodlit, breezily,
Galefully, Baltically cold with royal
Lashings of tat and Hey-Jimmy wigs, high on swigs
Of spinsterish, unmarried malt;
City of singletons, salt
Of the tilled earth, castled, unqueened, unkinged
Capital of no one knows what yet, bankers'
Losses mounting your besieged
Acropolises, the Waverley snow
Spattering on Sir Walter's deerhound, agley
This way and that, on the black cat
Crossing the kirkyard, the cartoon lassie
With the silver tassie, the boy
With a toy gun gunning for Covenanters,
The carlin ranting by the Water of Leith, the filed, billable teeth
Of lawyers, not proven under a barefaced cheek
Of chloroform, high-tea sunsets, Jennerdoms of discreetest passion,
Lace curtains drawn over mooning cannonballs, randy as the
    barrel of Mons Meg,
All brass bells unpolished, Magdalenism, Darwinian butchery,
Knox-talk, broderie, Brodies, bestial vennels,
Drug deals done under far too many bridges,
Midges, lost Provosts, the whole Botanic jing-bang,
Rhododendrons and ducks, fresh pasta and spliced Paolozzis,
Ramparts, rampant kirks, laddies' and ladies' hat-works,
David Humery, domes with hearty, clarty splashings,

The crowned spire, the dungeons, the crags, the old lags, the
  seagulls
Raucous on carless early mornings, the Firth of Forth perjink
  past crowsteps
Of informatics, draughty parallelograms, pandas and heritage pubs,
Cannons pointing rudely down the Canongate, the New Town's trig
Windowboxes geraniumed for suffragettes' parades,
The Bioquarter, the Quartermile, the hanged, drawn, and
  quartered,
Halls, gardens, harpsichords, waterfalls, jiggings and jeggings,
Festivals, Days Estival with lawyers' clerks, and couthy, uncouth
  doctors,
Surgeons' Hall surgeons, the burked dead, the Fringe, the
  redheads,
Hoaxed hexes, Samhain dreamers, schemies,
Anaemic academics, to-die-for grass, strollers, statuesque stalkers
Capering on parade with fire-eaters, unicyclists, caber-tossers,
  pipes and drums
YouTubed ad infinitum, the heady, reikie breath, and the rush
  of breathless newbies
Just off the train and already never leaving.

BIGAMY

Edinburgh

I love you as the Castle loves its rock. I love
Each wet flower in your floral clock

And, nuzzling the drizzly flowers beneath
In the dark ravine of your Water of Leith,

I hunt your tattoo,
Peekaboo

Down your closes, mount
Your hills, ride in your park, count

Every bright light till you come
To Enlightenment after Enlightenment,

And afterwards lie still, sated with who you are,
Listing your festivals, North Star.

Glasgow

I love you as its banks love the Clyde, holding you
Till you overflow, shaped by you, upholding you

Just a chuckie-skim from heaven.
Love you even

21

As the Mackintoshes loved art,
Schooled by you, caressing you, every part by heart

Till we sing, a Govan Gaelic Choir. I love you as the Finnieston Crane
Loves lifting. I exalt you again,

Ring you in my arms. Love you as the Mitchell Library loves
each book.
With the palm-tree heat of the Kibble Palace, I kiss your
elbow's crook,

Your red swing coat and your Gilmorehill.
I always will.

MANDELBOX CITY

for my son

Geeky pibroch, 3-D Brussels lace,
Each grace note coded with recursive grace,
Grids of cloned fractals choreograph their bright,
Fiddly finesse into a country dance,
A Monsieur Benoit Mandelbrot's Delight.
Spin-out, star turn, kaleidoscopic *tanz*,
Designed by you, it sings, this *a per se*
Digital schottische of perfect symmetry,
Nirvana cubed, sly, pocket-size advanced
Study in trance, impossibility
That works, now, as you stride out through your city,
Block by block, day after Reikie day
Of geeky pibroch, 3-D Brussels lace,
Each grace note coded with recursive grace.

SAN ANDREAS

Quakeless, faulty hickorigrad, too long home of homosocial golf,
Captained by ex-military chaps who failed the course,
And course-setters, all mortar-boarded with digital swank:
Where there's a Will there's a Kate.
All-weather Mecca of mediaevalists, on your Middle Age high-rise
Leylines converge, or three do: North Street,
South Street and Market Street, each thrawnly cobbled with cars.
Opposite that restaurant a heretic was burned,
Brass gobstopper in his mouth.
Up that church tower a big gun was hauled
To bombard the righteous. In God's 'Reformation bombsite'
John Knox, Borges, and Mary Queen of Scots
Glare at a fish and chip shop.
Full-on, the pale, crucified cathedral
Oversees high seas among Greek and eroding coding,
QR codes, canapés and creels.
Debt-ridden, teetering forever on the edge
Of fiscal and non-fiscal cliffs,
Scholars gallop towards sunstroked sands,
Yowling their chill inspiration.
The Castle uncrumbles, saving itself,
Only just, from North Sea blues,
Smug about its pioneer photographers,
Vestiges, Sir Kaleidoscope, sleet.
Even on a bad day you can spot a heron
Near the Rock and Spindle, or nab a poet
Or the ghost of one, in a dwam on The Scores;
On good days, precisely aligned as lasers,
Pipes and choir fling grace notes from the organ-loft.
Nothing happens here, six hundred times,
The six-hundred-and-first: *Eureka!*
Yahs and Wee Fionas, Amurkns, Shanghai connoisseurs,

Pilgrims from Tokyo with clubs
Traipse past scarlet-gowned pier reviews,
Ogle an Art-Deco cinema, a Byre
No cow was milked in, far too many pubs,
And Scots fall in love with it – not quite our country –
Half out of this world, half philosophically shat-on
By seagulls and journalists, half irreplaceable,
A one-off one-and-a-half:
Global village, Herculanaeum-on-Sea.
Not from here, I call it home.

ALMA MATER

If you went there from the mirrorglass,
Numbered spreadsheet streets of New York City,

If you took a plane, another plane,
A bus, and then a train, and then a bus

Out to that whetted edge, those salted cobbles,
It would be special for you only with

Stony resilience, creels, a gaunt horizon,
Its greatest treasures seaweed and a kiss,

And you would miss the young, despite the young
Jostling around you, fresher-faced, echoic,

Crowding like logarithms on a page
Turned over, checking one another out;

But now and then a word – matriculation,
Epistemology, Salvator, raisin –

Or a name you knew you knew, the name of someone
Burned alive out in the public street,

Would do its work and make you wish you'd worked
Harder, or differently, or not at all.

Time to go. And so you'd go again,
Clutching that phone you did not have before,

So many bags, but nothing to declare,
Nothing to scare the wary airport scanners,

Although you'd know for sure that you had on you
Something to smuggle back, a risk, a gift.

MANHATTAN

The rich live and work
Inside smart cell-phones, fifty,
Sixty storeys high.

*

In elevators
Descending through shafts, workers
Scroll down through their lives.

CAMBUS

Here, middle-class above the steelworks,
By that lang, slow bend, that cambus on the river,
Perched above molten Clydebridge,
Stood my capital of lentil-pathed gardens on tea trays
Flaunted at flower shows in the grey-sandstone Institute,
High castes tiered in prim geological strata
Above the Main Street, cast-offs below
Almost untouchable, a class Cold War
In that ex-pea-souped, still phlegm-spitting village
Fallen in the 60s towards a suburb,
Tabernacled, car-showroomed, bowling-greened with well-
    clicked jacks,
With its Preaching Braes, its Library fishtank and poetry,
Its Wark whose braw American evangelist
Orated to hordes in the park.
Swings chained on Sundays, Sabbaths of Thou Shalt Not Mow,
Trellised with roses, accountancy and righteousness,
Porn mags, Jags, and Rover 2000s,
Minis (though seldom with legs).
Long, crayon-coloured streets: Greenlees Road, Brownside Road
Dribbled with Cambuslang French – 'Chatelherault'.
Here I was cured by a tipsy doctor;
Nourished by a sawdust-floored butcher; sat,
Snapped, on a piano stool; biked down Douglas Drive
For cones and raspberry, sherbet dabs, and the sheer
Downhill rush of air down West Coats Road.
Omphalos of school uniforms, graveyard of far-flung school caps,
Its shopping-centre fountains always turned off to stop paddling,
Walls chalked with CUMBIE, hedges rife with dens
And occasional flashers, its Vesuvius a pit-bing,
Its pampas grass, like my parents, everlasting
With the rag-and-bone man whose hackit, blinkered horse

Summed up the place, like the slim kirk high on Kirkhill,
Hidden under no bushel, the swig, and the sneaked cigarette.
My oldest Cambuslang friend has had three strokes now. I was
  christened by the dead.
I cannot go back, but go back often at night
To those avenues of Harry Lauder, that place that could not lie
In its plain-ness, its secretly-listened-to Penderecki,
Its miners' boots and chemist's-shop, privet-lined calm,
To where it lies still by that lang, slow bend on the Clyde,
By new estates and Celtic knots of flyovers,
That bypassed zone, proud not to be Disneyfied like Rutherglen
Town Hall, but gobbled up by Glasgow, then spat back out
  again, indigestible,
Into red-roaded Lanarkshire, whose back-roads are now all
  tarred black.

SHETLAND

for Mary Blance

From the highest rock at the top of the hill
To the lowest stone in the ebb,

At Lunna Kirk by whose pews pipelines
Knit gas to Sullom Voe,

Through the islands' simmer dim
Glaciated grass still swoons,

Rising and birling under a gale
Of unleashed fiddlers' reels that sweep

From the highest rock at the top of the hill
To the lowest stone in the ebb.

GRAMPS

Nordic blue zoo of Super Pumas.
Men, but few women, in high-viz jackets
Or life jackets, strap themselves in.
Incomers head for the birch-draped book-cube,
A kickabout with tough, undonnish Dons,
Black gold, or the barn-like Kirk.
Fit like? On a good day, a bouclé of stone's
Diamondiferous deadweight shimmers,
But, under cloud, Union Street's ex-unionist grey
Dunts the cold soul; Dantescan docks
Slog non-stop, staving off hellfire heritage
With containers, fulmar spit, pelagic smells
Trolling granite spires of neo-Latinists
And the drip drip cash-seep of oil.
Doric columns march through this boreal Texas
Of fly-fishing, this sullen, Arctic Mons Graupius
Of manses, thrawn dynasties of dominies,
And rhyming couples cross-stitched in Duthie Park;
Few students now know which king
King's College is called after, or why
Bishop Elphinstone lies out in the rain.
Near the mediaeval makar's
'Ah, fredome is a nobil thing'
Money still talks — not always listened to;
Circus tents, pitched on billowy links,
Lend trapeze glee and levitation
To yoga-ish, auroral summer nights.
Portered by Angus-fed Shore Porters,
Since Tacitus, history's been drilled
Into by researchers for genetic markers, geo-phys, analysts
Of breviaries and Hector Boece.
Erasmus knew it as *Aberdonia*,

Reiver Margaret Thatcher as loot.
Fluvially decent, Dee and Don
Add to its municipal silver
Those other silvers, their liquid Oslo
Pure, distilled in tourist brochures, never
North enough, streaming way, way beyond
Forever and ever. Amen.

INTER-ISLAND CAUSEWAY

This small stretch of road
Is a horizontal prayer
As the climate shifts.

DISCOVERY

Marmaladegrad, old school of jam, jute, and journalism,
Fons et origo of *The Beano*;
Once William Wallace and Robert Fergusson
Learned Latin and premature death here.
Neared from the north between earth-houses,
Foxes' dens and runnels of snow;
From the south across Poet and Tragedian
William Topaz McGonagall's
Tay Bridge over homicidal waves,
Love-and-hate-knuckled conceptual-artville, exiling
A. L. from Kennedy, Herbert from W. N.,
Don from Professor Paterson,
Split self, groggy nurturer of painters' painters,
David Foggie, Dutch Davidson, McIntosh Patrick,
Home ground of nil-nil and Desperate also-ran Dan,
Auld dominies' *Dei donum*, God's gift to medical research,
Hard grafter of genetics, hotspot of Kuma and Gehry,
City 'greater than the pyramids of Memphis',
Caster of bread on greedy waters'
Silvery, reed-bedded Firth, investor
In haar, admiral of sandbanks, ruler
Of a backyard Raj, your very own Verdant Works
Mad for the Magdalen Green; Mary Shelley's
Whaleopolis, city of winter cumulus,
Beached *Discovery*, CAD, DCA, and V&A light,
Your nightlife all birdlife, songs and tweeted snogs,
Bleary veteran of virtual reality and backhanders,
No one unDundonian adores you. You're loved
More stubbornly than pehs by lads from the Hilltown
Under their mammies' thumbs, and by nippy
Outlaws off Law Hill, and sleek, professorial policewomen
Thirled to their screens, cold cynosure of gairfish,

Your team Disunited, dour diva with imperfect pitch,
Beery detester of Winston Churchill,
Cubbyhole of artists' books,
Rig-builder, riven with bandstand surprises,
Begetter of the 'Ode to Tesco' and 'Dundee salad' (meaning chips),
Hotspot of Dundee cake, town twinned with Crocodile Dundee,
Your D. C. Thomson out-bossing Washington, D.C.,
So many lives drawn up from your Nine Wells
Have trudged down Peep o' Day Lane,
Launch-site of the Good and Godly Ballads,
Oncologists' baronial bolthole, home port of gamers. Eh? Eh?
Your dream job: to be misunderstood.

HOME

The dark universe
Is full of candles, burning
For our safe return.

PORT

Berth-place of John Galt, birthplace
Of James Watt whose surname named watts,
Slave money over-sweetening your sandstone tenements,
Black GIs from Missouri wowed by your tainted Firth
As they packed railway carriages jammed along long Princes Pier,
Over for D-Day, standing at troop-train windows,
Bemused and smiling to sweet-starved white kids who yelled,
'Any gum, chum?' till packets were thumb-flicked across.
Sea town of the blitzed girl blown upstairs
By high explosives, of the doilied dolls' tea party
Under the kitchen table to a Luftwaffe whistle of bombs
That pause in mid-air while time stops, and dark rings of guns
Round Kirn pound the skies, then the night goes red
With burning whisky, blazing streets napalmed with malt.
Mustering point of mariners, submariners, Jamiesons,
Campbells and seen-it-all, ocean-going clans –
Free French, Poles, Canadians – they line up, assemble, draw breath,
Back-from-the-dead riveters, Stanley Spencered by gantries
At Port Glasgow, teeming from your graveyard shifts
With tools and tool bags, sprucing yourselves up, Comet-
Launcher where the burned-out outdo the living, Cloch-watcher,
Drydock of soft, apocalyptic rain. Through you,
Paradisal dump, persist less the names
Highland Mary, W. S. Graham, or A. Dunn, Bookseller,
Than just the word GREENOCK, its sunstruck, meandering Cut
Incised into Scotland, that thin canal of primroses,
Sunshine and hot walks over the moors to Wemyss Bay,
O slipway of too many ships, battered esplanade,
Your Lyle Road still a panorama of Nirvana,
A hand-stitched prinking of yachts past the Tail of the Bank;
Home to the wee girl whose dad said, 'Tell your teacher
"I'm a MacLean of Duart. We had our own boat at the Flood."'

Only begetter of the Tontine Hotel, godfather of the Atlantic
  Gulf Stream,
Mother of all voyages out,
Born survivor, bonny fechter, breath
Of fresh, salt air, your people heirs apparent to Popeye
And the *Jeanie Deans*, recession-hit binnacle, druggy
Star port, cosmopolitan with gangways,
Ghost Cunarders and ferries, livewire ready for the ferryman
Whenever he comes, with the summer's day litany of your crossing:
Kirn, Dunoon, Innellan, Rothesay, the Firth of Styx.

DRAGONFLY

How can Iona
Tell the peerless dragonfly,
'You've one day to live'?

ALZHEIMER'S

I am the only one now who remembers,
Snug in the darkness of my mother's hatbox,
Her favourite hat, sculpted from weightless feathers,
So rarely worn, still fit for summer weddings,
A deep blue bird, waiting to fly the nest.

MILKING SONG

Pee the milk, dearie,
Pee it on and on,
Pee the milk, dearie,
Until the milk is gone.

Where stringy paths curl
Among wood sorrel
Past lovers
And golden plovers,
Kisses tasting of pears
And leaping hares,
Dirty lochs,
Brochs,
Containerisation
And pasteurisation,
Lochans
And supermarket cartons,
Brown cows
And Mao,
Village pond
And International Monetary Fund,
Stamina
And famine,
Psalters,
Defaulters,
Byres
And buyers,
Crowdie
And dry powder,
Charms
And abandoned farms . . .

Pee the milk, dearie,
Pee it on and on,
Pee the milk, dearie,
Until the milk is gone.

YOUNG POET

The schoolteacher's scratchy pen records an absence;
Streets away, eyes averted from a textbook,
One foot on the ground and one foot off it,
A boy sits, picking fleas off a dog.

DRAWING

The miracle is,
Taking a line for a walk,
You know where to go,

And, like a mirror
Turned window, here you author
Your clear, one-page book.

ARCHILOCHOS

young nightingales

*

fig

between the thighs

*

kingfisher's wingbeats

faster and faster

*

engorging lots

of blind eels

*

Balled below my heart, desire for love
fogged my eyes, ripped my breath away, clawed
the soft lungs right out of my chest

ALKAIOS

... no ... I ...

*

... I was ...

*

... Alkaios ...

*

as if drawing from the grey sea ...

*

... submerged places ...

*

... signs, constellations ...

*

... ownerless ...

*

... when you save them as they perish ...

*

... they would become ...

ECHO CHAMBER

Fleerish fleerishes:
But nae jo
Tae enjose it wi.

Fleerish faas:
But nae jo
Tae blirt wi.

Ah speir
Jist whan loo's ee
Jummles us maist —

Whan fleerish fleerishes,
An aa
Whan fleerish faas.

★

Midnicht. The mune sets wi the Seiven Sisters.
The oors gang by. I lig awake. Alane.

Blossom blossoms: but there is no sweetheart with whom to enjoy it. Blossom falls: but there is no sweetheart with whom to mourn it. I ask just when love's craving agitates us most — when blossom blossoms, and also when blossom falls.

★

Midnight. The moon sets with the Pleiades. The hours go by. I lie awake. Alone.

(after Xue Tao and Sappho)

Ach, Orpheus,
Abune his heid fleed countless burds. The fush
Flang theirsels up oot o the daurk-blae wattirs
Jist for the drap-deid brawness o his sang.

*

Afore ma lair
Yon munelicht's
Bricht
Lik rind.

Raxin up ma heid
Ah tak tent o thi fite fu mune,
An, joukin ma heid,
Drame Ah'm hame.

Oh, Orpheus: above his head flew countless birds. The fish flung themselves up out of the dark-blue waters simply for the drop-dead beauty of his song.
*

In front of my bed that light of the moon is bright like frost. Raising my head, I pay attention to the white full moon, and, bowing my head, dream I'm home.

(after Simonides and Li Bai)

48

At the peep o Mairch,
Pussywillows —
Licht an free;

A saft Mairch wind
Maks thaim waffle
An taisle fowk's claithes.

The pussywillows o yon hoose,
In sense,
Are jist ajee:

Eftir hechtin
Tae flicht sooth,
They flicht aff nor.

★

halie   oracle   yoam   flichtin awa

*At the opening of March, catkins — light and free; a gentle March wind makes them
wave about and tease people's clothing. The catkins of that house, in essence, are
simply unstable: after promising to fly south, they fly off north.*

★

holy   oracle   fragrant   fleeing

(after Xue Tao and Simonides)

Ootlin, tell oor maisters this:
We lig here deid. We did as we were telt.

*

Tuim bens. Naebdy kythin.
Jist vices echoin –
An licht hame-comin tae ilka daurk fir,
The strath's tap bricht aince again.

Stranger, take this message to our masters: we lie here dead. We did as we were told.

*

Empty mountains. Nobody in evidence. Only voices echoing – and light returning to each dark fir, the top of the water meadow bright again.

(after Simonides and Wang Wei)

Aince I tuik fush fae Argos tae Tegea,
A queer creel oan ma shouders. But nae mair.

*

We pairt, an Ah see fae yon heich broch
The Wattir blink i the gloamin;
Day-set; corbies flichterin hame;
The traiveller stravaigin awa.

*Once I used to carry fish from Argos to Tegea, a strange creel on my shoulders, but I
do so no longer.*

*

*We part, and I see from that high tower the River shine in the twilight; sunset; ravens
flying home; the traveller wandering away.*

(after Simonides and Wang Wei)

Bidin for a canny moment,
Its totie sowl
Is a cleek,

An, neist, a fan
Fae a Han luim –
Roon,

Siller-glancie,
Its state
Growin dowily
Heavy o the fit.

Hoo monie fowk
Hae had a care
O Lochiel's lantern
Fae quarter tae fu?

*

Frien, this is nae grand laird's mausoleum.
A puir yin needs nae big lair. This'll dae.

Waiting for a moment to be born, its tiny spirit is a hook; and, next, a fan from a Han loom – round, silver-shining, its disposition growing sadly pregnant. How many people have kept watch over the moon from crescent-moon to full?

*

Friend, this is no great lord's tomb. A poor person does not require a big tomb. This one will do.

(after Xue Tao and Simonides)

THE SCOTTISH AMBASSADOR

Still loyal to our European partners
But fascinated by the Sassenachs,

Dressed in my ceremonial regalia,
It takes so long to jink through the jostling streets

That, tired out since the day I first came down
Here to the thronged South Bank, I started sneezing

At yon billowing acrid smell of burning timbers
From the lost Globe Theatre; then,

After the king's head bounced and the dome rose,
Crossing the Thames, I glimpsed our man of substance,

Davie Hume, historian of England;
But, slipping past and whisked along The Mall

Through imperial crowds in corsets and top hats,
Combat fatigues and diesel fumes and hotpants,

Then, lastly, pushing through a line of earpieced
Flunkeys scanning apps and texting lists,

Reaching my grand, historic destination,
I'm struck now how the monarch in the flesh

Seems flat-pack ordinary, and half flinches
When, with the Braveheart glimmer of a smile,

I bide my time and in a measured way
Bow, then present my credentials.

ACKNOWLEDGEMENTS

Some of these poems first appeared in *Archipelago*, *The Book of Iona* (Polygon, 2016), *The Caught Habits of Language* (ed. Rachael Boast and Andy Ching, Donut Press, 2018), *Chinese Makars* (Easel Press, 2015), *Cities* (Clutag Press Five Poems Series, No. 6, 2016), *Fire* (Hirundo Press, 2017), *Light Box* (Easel Press, 2015), *London Review of Books*, *Simonides* (Easel Press, 2011), and *The Scores*.

Thanks are due also to the artists Norman McBeath, Leena Nammari, and Caroline Saltzwedel with whom I worked on several of the above publications; to Alice Crawford, Aisha Farr, David Godwin, David Kinloch, Garry MacKenzie, Song Da, and Xi Zhao; to all members of the Loch Computer network, sponsored by the Royal Society of Edinburgh; to Edinburgh Printmakers, the Scottish Poetry Library, and the University of St Andrews for commissions; and to Robin Robertson for editorial shrewdness.